Celestial Dreams

Visits from Heaven

Brandan Arthur Bennett

Made with ❤ on the BookLeaf Publishing Platform
www.bookleafpub.in
www.bookleafpub.com

Dedication

Dedicated to all those above and below. Still always with you. Always with and from love from Heaven above.

Preface

Ever since I was a boy I would get visits from ones who have passed over, messages from loved ones for their loved ones and just lots of fun times and experiances. Here is a few that really stand out to me. Shared into a collection of poems for you to enjoy and I to remember.

Acknowledgements

I thank all those who listend and recieved with open
arms, tearful eyes, smiles so bright and love filled hearts.
All those souls who were waiting to go or trying to move
on. The one who just came on visitors pass. To all the
loved ones who watch and guide us on our crazy lives.
To those who trusted and recieved no matter what their
belief. To all those on the other side who came, sorry but
way to many to name. But most of all to God for the gift
and courage to share. Thank you Jesus!
Faith and Trust. It all works out and we all get there
when we get there.

E + B =  2

I love and thank my family ♥ 🕊️ 😇

1. Lady in the green dress

It was a special date

No time to be late

Fancy curls

Looking forward to Ballroom twirls

Prettiest green dress

It was the only one she owend

Like a queen she glistend sitting on her thrown

She had a gorgeous glow

In her hair a pretty bow

The two men came to pick her up

They had a fancy pick up truck

Like a 44 Ford

Oh Lord

It was heaven sent

I didn't know what it all ment

But two days earlier she had just past

It happened so fast

I rushed off to tell my friend

For the lady was the grandma of his lovely wife

The one who cared for her all her life
Those two men who escorted her home
One of family and one to be wed
Well they were both already dead
Waiting to pick her up again
After that special day and special dance
After her life had passed
After it had it's last chance
Back to our Celestial Dome
With God and family in our forever home

2. Dumpster Girl

It was a sad night
My dreams fiiled with fear
Hard and heavy
It felt like a title fight
I had no idea there was a deal
At that time I never took the kneel
No idea she was so near
I couldn't undertand crystal clear
She had asked for help
Said it wasn't their fault
They put her body in the garbage bin
Behind the 7/11
With the store that sold the yummy maults
Oh Angels of Heaven
They didn't mean to
She slipped in the bath
To much time had past
It became her last
Her very last breath
Parents hooked on meth

Panic sunk in
They didnt know where to begin
Strikened with fear and no where to run
Relazing what they had done
They placed her in the garbage bin
Reported that she was lost
Kidnapped, please help us at whatever the cost
But little did they know
Days later I saw the answers on a televison show
It's called the news
In those days inbetween
She came to me a few times
Always when I snoozed
She was found by the garabage man
Man, I didn't know
I didn't know what todo
I had no clue
I tried the best I can
But I doubted if it was even true
So much in my head
But in reality this little girl was dead
Later justice was taken
But I sure was shaken
She found her piece
Up and away she went
For me it surly was a lesson
And a very special blessing

Along with so much more
No other explination
But Heaven sent
And there she went
Back through Heaven's door
Thank you Dumpster Girl
So cute with her little hair in braids
Those fancy beutiful curls
I'm sorry if I prolonged your stay
I just didn't know how or what to say

3. He just wanted to watch TV and its about to rain

I was about 23
I didn't know what was inside me
Thoughts in my head
Really?
Messages and visits from the dead
The work day ended
I was very tired
It was time to retire
To sleep I went
Let the talking begin
"It's about to rain and he wants to come in"
I said in my sleep
As I rolled in my slumber
Then it began to thunder
Sure enough it started to rain
Awake or asleep at times it feels insane
The TV turns on
There was no more fear
He is actually always near

He was where he belonged
He came for a visit
Time to realax and just sit
To get out of the rain
Perhaps ease the pain
Clear the confusion
It wasn't a spirit intrusion
I remembered it was my Grandpa's birthday
He was just popping in not much to say
Just to spread his love
Cause thats what Grandpas do
A special visitor's pass from Heaven above
I'll try my best to match your glow
I love you always Abuelito

4. The AA Dream Team

Well years had past
I had gotten much older
I learned I would carry the message pain in my shoulder
That is until I deliver
But this time
Well this time I had fear
So much it made me quiver
I didn't know all who was near
I still doudted and lacked in trust
But follwing Gods orders
I knew I had to do what I must
It's how the poems began
So I wrote and heard what the angels sang
What they told and shared
When I shared
I got alot of amazed stares
There was more then twelve
One by one they all got delivered
Like I was picked off a shelve
I realized I had been chosen

I never felt bigger
I felt so spirtually strong
I love when they communicate through song
It helped them but it helped me believe
Relaized the purpose for what I hear and see
Gifted with a special gift
Even if I was or am a misfit
It comes from God's love
His enternal protection
Blessed are we
That is love is an a infection
He helped me see
Helped me uderstand
It is all part of the Celestial plan
So I will try my best
To always do what I can
And trust Father that you'll giving a lending hand
I love you and thank you
It truly all comes from above

5. This is what awaits

Well about a year had past
My first marriage didn't last
She had passed away
Both of us only 36
Still so much life to live
Still so much to say
But there wasn't another day
One night full of doubt
Sitting in my sorrow
I still had no idea what life was all about
I said good night to the kids
See you all tomoorow
To sleep I went
Then she came Heaven sent
I could see her
I could smell her
But I couldn't feel her
She told me many things
Many things about that special place
I was still memorzied just to see her beutiful face

To see that pretty smile
To hear her uniquie voice
She said "we all have the choice"
"It's like walking a very long mile"
She said "stay faithful this is what awaits"
Then she opened a window
A window to the promise the land
So many colors so many Saints
More then a artist could paint
More then crayola has in a box
So happy and giddy like a fox
A bleaming bold and bright glow
I didn't know to stay or to go
Just to dive right in
After all it's where life begins
It was inviting and warm
A peace I felt before
She grabbed me by the hand
Told me she loved me
To trust in Father's plan
Hoped I could undertand
I was sad when I awoke
But wow what a night
Knowing we have help on this Earthly fight
To help us get there
To help us challenge
To overcome the dare

I thank you God for all the insight
For all the visitis of all those who came
Some visits are short and some are long
See you again Steph
Love you forever and beyond

6. She likey the drug

Growing up in Ute land
I always felt they had a helping hand
Always felt they were around
But they rairly made a sound
I played with them as a boy
Young imagination and mountain toys
I found artifcats and arrowheads
Made rattles and drums
Visions and dreams filled my head
I had many more visits from the dead
But they were my friends
Much time in life had passed
I became much older in age
I still love the smell of their sage
I took my love for a hike in Boulder
To go through the Royal Arch
Flowers were blooming
It was a little after March
Perhaps they are like portals
For angels and us mortals

Well later to sleep I went
That night Shavano was sent
I already new his name
He still even looked the same
Standing over my love
By the edge of the bed
So present and so visual
Was he even dead
What's the deal
Waving his hands
I thought is this even real
He said give her a snake bite
He showed me with his hands
The venom would clear out the drug
Then poof he went like a shake of a rug
Just to deliver what was sent
What was needed
I gave my love a big hug
Told her I love her so much
So I pleaded and pleaded
Told her lets go catch a snake
Just one bite
I dont think it's a mistake
Well back to bed
I love you and good night

7. Still Open

Oh Ms Laura
The unusal proncuing of your name
This time it wouldn't be me who thought they were
insane
She worked in the lounge
She hated staying late
"Still open" she would mudder and say
But on one special day
Well her brother finally came
He had passed on
He had done horrbile things
Violent and abusive
Stole jewelry and pretty rings
He came to say he was sorry
That he had made amends
He was sorry for hurting family & friends
That he had found Jesus
That he was hopeful for his sister and mother too
He said "ask the cleaner"
"He has a specil gift for you"

Well earlier that day
Meetings with the Missionaries
Sharing spirtual testimonies
So true so sweet
Like delcious blueberries
I decided to take the leap
I felt prompted to bring the good book
But the one I grabbed when I took a look
Oops its El Libro de Mormon
Spanish version
So I left it behind
I didn't see the sign
I'm such a block head
Laura being from Mexico
Spanish her first langauge
It was a book she had never read
How could've I messed this up
Let the messages get so entangled
When she shared and asked
"You have something for me"
Then I could truly see
This one wasn't just for her but also me
That no matter what to try
The next day she got her book
Then the next day she quit
I can be such a dimwit
But it is what it took

For me to learn
For me to see
That he gives us all turn
That Jesus loves me
Thay he loves all of us
A chance to return home
With our loved ones in that Celestial dome

8. Gabriel's flight

Have you ever wanted to be like
Peter Pan
To go on a night time flight
Well a ride along with Gabriel
can
Don't be frightened
Angles are pretty tough
They can look a little rough
Just hold on tight
You might just get enlightened

Up up and away
That sure was a special day

9. A silly break

BOOM BAM WOW

HOLLY KAZO

KITSCABODDLE

FAT ON STRUDDLE

WHAM BAM

SHAZAM

CAPTAIN CHAOS

AMEDEUS AMEDUES

OH OH AMEDEUES

A SIMPLE MENTAL BREAK

GO WALK A MILE

SIT AND SMILE

PONDER AND WANDER
THEN BACK AGAIN
CAUSE MY FRIEND
IT NEVER ENDS

10. Tell him I made up with Dad

Oh neighbor Steve

Sorry your Bro had to
leave

One cool cat he was

One chill angel he is

Told me about his life

Like it was a moive in
show biz

So in all his grace
All his glory
I had to share his story
You should of seen
Steve's face
Once I finally shared
But once I said
"Oh wait, he wanted to
tell you. He made up with
dad"
Well for 30 plus years
They didn't speak to each

other
Both so mad
Not a word to his dad all
through his brother
It didn't matter how
much time had past
Tell that day he rode his
motorcycle to fast
That's the day Steve lost
his brother
Back to Heaven with his
Father and Mother

11. Oh Mel

OH THE ANGEL MEL

MELCHIZEDECK IS HIS NAME

*ANGEL S**T HIS GAME*

BONSAI

12. Olive the Potter

Genetation to genetation like to create with clay
Some for work some for play
My Granny B
Well she would always take me
The Wee Ones, that was the place
You should of seen me face
40 years later after the passing of Olive Waltz
Well banks get ready to open the vaults
Another great business is in the plan
Even though I didn't believe I can
Even though I didn't believe what I was told
You see I was gifted all her pottery molds
But long before Olive's last dance
i was told I would have the chance
For a place for families to heal and create
So save the date
Love Duck is coming
I just never liked running
So I took the longway
I took my time

Now I can cash in all the dimes
Know I can open any day
Yeah I love to play with clay

13. Theresa and the kids

Running, laughing, skipping and singing
That is what all these children did
The only thing was they were all dead
Some call them energy some call them ghost
When I clean is when I see them the most
Spirits still hear
Oh my dears
I asked why
I didn't know how what to try
Let alone what to do
I mean I know alot of spirtual stuff
But I don't do Quiji boards or Voodo
Jesus is my man
The one true king
Heaven sent
I just didn't know what it all ment
So I let the children play
They would peek and poke
Follow me around while I clean
They weren't scary or mean

Then I asked alot questions
To help with my confusion
Them she appeared it was like a angel came
I asked what is your name
A velvet heart flutted out of the trash
The name embroided on it said Theresa
I said well nice to meet ya
She was the nurse mother
Lots of the children were sisters or brothers
The place was a 1800s orphanige for children who lost it
all in the civi war
I was a little shaken even struck to the core
Theresa just kept them safe
Ailve and dead
It was so real and visual I knew it wasn't in my head
She helped them tell some one opened Heaven's door
Well I guess that was me as I cleaned and mopped the
floor
Thank you Clayton Campus Kids
I'm thankful for what I did

14. To love and love again

There she was 15 sitting on her friend's bed looking hot
Me and the boys coming by to smoke some pot
Oh she was super cute
She even played the flute
Well a few years past
Now I was 19 and she 18
She was still so pretty she looked like a beauty queen
I mustard some courage and went in for kiss
It was like fireworks galore
The feeling was magical I knew I wanted more
So we had lots of fun
Had lots of great teenage sex
Started to get serious and I was falling in love
Had no idea what was coming next
But God had other plans
He already knew his plan from above
So like a dove away she flew
Over a 1,000 miles away
Coudn't ride my bike that far
I had no driver license so I coudn't drive a car

I had no clue what todo
Over 20 years had passed
Then she called my name
She had so many thoughs of me she felt she was going
insane
She picked up the phone and gave it a rang
I thought oh yeah you just remebered my wang
Boom boom baby yeah
But she remembed it all
How when she was on my bike handlebars I wouldnt let
her fall
How I would make fer feel safe
How I can put a smile on her face
Make her laugh and giggle
She even would go to gym with me and let her flubber
jiggle
Just kidding no flubber
I just put that in
So she would say "hey" when she read it
But always being a great cuddler
I jumped right in
Elizabeth is back again
Well now we're Husband & Wife
Looks like I've loved her my entire life
Love did come back again
But it reality love never left
Are hearts still had that tingle

Boy am I forever thankful
She picked up the phone and gave me a jingle
I love you Elizabeth Marie Bennett
Thank you for marrying me

15. Isiaha,Oh wait it's Eziaha

Night time school janitor
You can hear alot of bantor
Alot of things that go bump in
the night
Aftermath of a playground fist
fight
But this time I heard a voice
As I vacumed and cleaned
For what seemeed like days I
heard it scream
Isiaha , Isiaha, Isiaha
It was hard to make clear

I just felt a little girl near
Well my time was done
I had hired staff
Almost two years went bye
I was so busy and unware I didn't
even try
Try to help or try resolve
I assuemd with time the thoughts
and feelings would disolve
Then came a different school
further south in a whole different
city
Sure enough I was cleaning again
Then I heard that voice
I recogonozed it like a friend
But this time understood no

question wheter I was insane
Eziaha Eziaha is her name
She came to tell her mom and
dad
That she was happy and glad
That it wasn't their fault
That they did they all they could
That she loved them so much
That she was with them always
It was a special day for all of us
Parents their daughter and I
We all learned so much that day
After I didn't have much else to
say
Few days later I was fired
But it was ok I was tired

After all I had carried that
message for years
Eziaha had to stay close hold
back her tears
Had to overcome her fears
Her parnets had taught at the
first school I heard her voice
After I had left that place with
the message stll unclear
They moved south to Colorado
Springs to a school that was no
where near
But God's work is everywhere he
finds the way
So he decided that was the day
After that I never herd from

Eziaha again

But I do know when I get there I
already have a special friend

16. Uncle Bob wants you to fish

Perry was a young lad
Still under 20
A Missionary for the Latter Day Saints
Perry was sad
Gospel work well he did plenty
What I shared with him almost made him faint
He and his companion where at my house
When all of sudden it came to me
Fast and clear more real then Mickey Mouse
Well you see
Uncle Bob was dead
But his message for his nephew was in my head
I shouted "your Uncle Robert wants you to finish your
mission then move to Alaska to operate his fishing boat"
Well y'all
You see prior Perry had alot of doubt
Unsure of what was next
He knew he always tried his best
As for Uncle Bob well he died before Perry's 2 years

Before he went and spread Christ's love
Can't you see, see that they are near
That they watch and guide from above
That was a special day for my missionary friend and I
That was the day I relaized I didn't even have to try
That when it is from God above
When it comes from Love
That it just flows wihtout thinking
As for Perry what ever ocean or lake he is at
I hope he is fishing and his boat isn't sinking

17. Grandma wants you to
change the world

It was back at DIA again
Actually back when it all began
I was told give her the stone
The first one you see
She will be on her knees
There she was tying her shoe
She was on a new adventure
Leaving home she felt alone
Afriad of something new
Her sweet grandma from above
So strong and very proud
The message was cryastsl clear
Her voice so loud
Heaven's light shining on her so bright
So I gathered up my might
I let the message flow
I gave her the rock
And wouldn't you know
It was both their birthstone

She wasn't alone
Off to teach and heal kids
Shape and protect their minds
Her and Grandma are a rare special kind

18. You just need to learn to listen

Bing Clung Cling Clong
Okay ding dong
Noises in the head
Voices of the dead
Since you were a boy
No it's not a toy
It's a special gift
Wether the top of the elite
Or the number 1 misfit
You have your mission
Only 1 option and it's not defeat

You just need to learn to listen

That is what Great Granny said

That is what I'll do

Keep trying

Trying my best

In this life and long after I'm dead

Listen to the voices in my head

Do what is asked and get the

needed rest

19. Hope

🎵🎶🎵 Joy 🎶🎶🎵

JOY TO ALL THE WORLD

That is hope

That the world finds peace

That Christ's Universal Love

rains down

That smiles will cross oceans

That laughter will roar like

thunder

That love will spread like wildfire

That HOPE will fill and grace

each season

No rhyme or reason
Just hope in humanity
To get through the clamaity
To just have hope

20. Don't touch the laundry machine

So I was asked to clean a house
This one for a dear friend
Her father's life came to a end
So I got my stuff and began
Boy the messages were deep
Loud & clear with a stuffed fish
for me to keep
Of all the things he had to say
He told me so many things that
day
But what was insctruced and

shouted
Was "don't touch the laundry
machine"
But the family doubted
Or maybe just forgot
Either way good thing I left
behind a mop
They started a luandry load
Even after they were told
Then the basement flooded
It wasn't crystal clear
More lightly muddled
"I told you so"
He will always be near
Thanks Jim for the experiance
and the fish

You will be missed

Onward we go

21. E+B= 2

Elizabeth Marie Bennett

Used to be a Kennedy

Then was Mrs Lavine

Well now she is all mine

I fell in love at nineteen

Took her to Grannys house

For a dinner with the Queen

Maybe it was a lunch

But she had a hunch

That now wasn't the time

But she was well worth the wait

So many years later now she is back

Prettier then ever

Boy I took the bait

Made her my wife

Now I have her forever

Angel right by my side

Along with me for the ride

E+B= ♥2

That's the special equation
Life with her is like a vacation
Once in a lifetime
Well read the rhyems
For the Bennett's it is everyday
Well I hope you enjoyed these collection of poems and
all I had to say

www.ingramcontent.com/pod-product-compliance
Lightning Source LLC
LaVergne TN
LVHW050936200726

843508LV00011B/2358